D1571365

Looking Back
LANE COUNTY

A PICTORIAL RETROSPECTIVE OF LANE COUNTY, OREGON: THE EARLY YEARS

PRESENTED BY

The Register-Guard

Acknowledgments

The Register-Guard is pleased to present "Looking Back, Lane County: The Early Years."

This unique book is the result of contributions made by many people and organizations from throughout the county.

We are indebted to early residents who captured their times – our history – in photographs. And we're all indebted to the many individuals who are committed to preserving our history in various libraries, archives and personal collections all around Lane County.

In addition to precious selections from family albums of many Register-Guard readers, we also received the generous contribution of time and photo archives from the Lane County Historical Museum, the Springfield Museum and the University of Oregon Knight Library. We also thank Christena Brooks, special publications writer for The Register-Guard Advertising Department, for writing the chapter introductions.

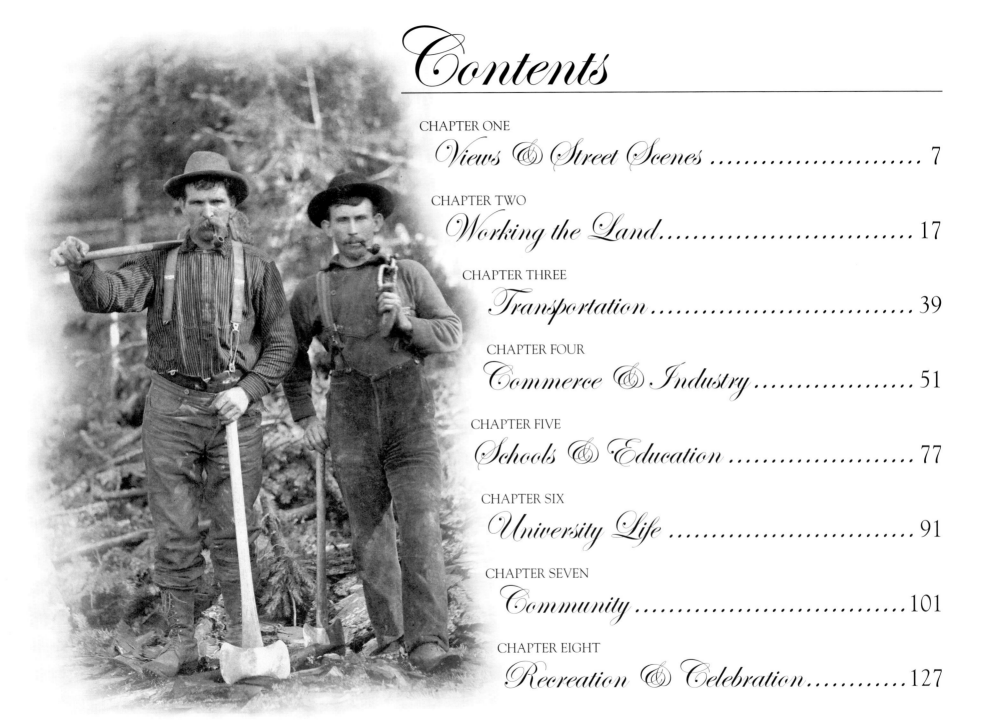

Contents

Foreword

We are pleased to bring you this pictorial retrospective of life in Lane County from the mid-1850s to the late 1930s. If it's true that a picture tells a thousand words, this book contains volumes.

These pictures don't presume to record the important moments of history. They merely offer glimpses of life, often everyday life, in Lane County, focusing on commerce and industry, agriculture, schools, sports, the University of Oregon, transportation, community groups and more.

In these pages readers will see in the faces of the county's early inhabitants their determination, resilience and sacrifice, and their unbridled pride in their young and growing community.

We want to thank the many local residents and organizations who shared priceless photos with us. This project would not have been possible without the generous participation of the Lane County Historical Museum, the Springfield Museum, and the UO Knight Library.

For 78 years, The Register-Guard has been a part of the lives of the people who call Lane County home. We're proud that our newspaper is a part of your life, whether its pages are unfolding at your breakfast table, billowing in the breeze on your front porch in summer, shared with loved ones before a crackling fire in winter or tucked securely under arm on the way to work.

Lane County has gone through many changes over the past 150 years, and The Register-Guard has changed, too. Our technology has evolved from letter-by-letter typesetting to today's offset printing with high-quality color photographs and advertising. But some things remain the same: a commitment to our local community, to friendly customer service and, above all, to be a trusted voice of news and information.

We hope you enjoy looking back at Lane County's early years.

Alton F. Baker III
Editor & Publisher

CHAPTER ONE

Views & Street Scenes

Suppose you could travel back in time to Lane County in the early 1900s. As you walk down the streets, you find few familiar sights. Here and there, though, is a recognizable home, tree or other landmark.

In Eugene, a conspicuously bald Skinner Butte overlooks the downtown train yard, which is busy with activity. Trains are still the most reliable way to bring goods in and out of town. Over in Springfield, Main Street is already an important thoroughfare through town; it goes by the original Southern Pacific Depot, built in 1891. In Florence, fishing vessels dot the ocean, while a new lighthouse at picturesque Heceta Head is manned by a full-time keeper.

These towns are young; their settlers arrived only half a century earlier. In 1846, Virginian Elijah Bristow was the first to stake a claim in future Lane County. He named the 640-acre site Pleasant Hill. Fellow adventurer Eugene F. Skinner staked his own claim next to the Willamette River near present-day Skinner Butte. Three years later, settler Elias Briggs built a cabin to the southeast and named it Springfield after a bubbling spring on the homestead.

Smaller towns, many of them built by lumber companies for their workers, can be found at far-flung locations throughout the county. On the city streets and rural roads, automobiles that were once the toys of the wealthy are becoming more common, but they still share the road with horses and buggies.

Eugene is jokingly referred to as Skinner's Mud Hole, a title that isn't completely undeserved due to regular flooding. Springfield and other cities don't escape that fate either; Glenwood, lowlands between the two cities, is so often submerged that residents are accustomed to fleeing to the UO campus when the water rises. Relief from nature's spring fury only comes when Congress passes the Flood Control Act and workers begin constructing an elaborate system of dams and reservoirs.

Left: A view of Willamette Street from 10th Avenue, Eugene, circa 1913. Ax Billy Department Store, whose sign hangs over the street, appears on the right. *Courtesy Lane County Historical Museum*

Right: View of the three bridges in Springfield, circa 1900. *Courtesy Springfield Museum*

Above: Willamette Street, looking south from 6th Avenue, Eugene, circa 1911. The Hampton building is on the right. *Courtesy Lane County Historical Museum*

Right: Willamette Street in Coburg, 1912. *Courtesy Lane County Historical Museum*

Above: View of Florence, taken from the south shore of the Siuslaw River. The public school with belfry is near the center of the photo. *Courtesy Lane County Historical Museum*

Above: View of Eugene, looking south up Willamette Street toward Spencer Butte, circa 1915.
Courtesy Lane County Historical Museum

Right: Street scene in the town of Blue River, located on the McKenzie River, circa 1920. The Blue River Hotel (also known as the Antler Inn) can be seen to the left of the photo. *Courtesy Lane County Historical Museum*

Above: Early view of Cottage Grove, circa 1915. *Courtesy Barbara Anheluk*

Left: Willamette Street looking north from 8th Avenue, Eugene, circa 1916.
Courtesy Lane County Historical Museum

Above: A view of Willamette Street in Eugene, looking north, circa 1926.
Courtesy Lane County Historical Museum

Left: View of Eugene, looking south up Willamette Street toward Spencer Butte, early 1920s.
Courtesy Lane County Historical Museum

Above: View of Florence, looking toward the Siuslaw River estuary, circa 1936. The Florence public school building can be seen in the foreground. *Courtesy Lane County Historical Museum*

Right: Seth Laraway Building at 980 Willamette Street, Eugene, circa 1927. *Courtesy Lane County Historical Museum*

Above: Main Street, Cottage Grove, circa 1939. Doleman's Bakery and Mountain Stages Power Company, 319 and 321 Main Street are on the right. *Courtesy Lane County Historical Museum*

Left: Broadway looking east towards the W.E. Miner Building, Eugene, 1926. Notice the Trail to Rail Pageant banner over the street. *Courtesy Lane County Historical Museum*

Above: View of Broadway between Oak and Pearl streets, Eugene, circa 1938. Quackenbush Hardware and Eugene Hotel can be seen on the south side of the street. *Courtesy Lane County Historical Museum*

Left: Heceta Head Lighthouse and keeper's dwellings, Lane County coast, circa 1939. Cape Creek tunnel entrance can be seen at the right. *Courtesy Lane County Historical Museum*

CHAPTER TWO
Working the Land

It's hard to believe that Lane County's first settlers weren't immediately aware of the financial opportunity awaiting them in Oregon's virgin forests. They were more concerned with finding fertile soil for farming. Between the Willamette and McKenzie rivers, they discovered a nutrient-rich bottomland capable of growing almost anything.

When the California Gold Rush hit, there was suddenly an insatiable demand for timber for the construction of gold mines. Oregon's southern neighbor bought lumber as fast as Lane County loggers could supply it, which wasn't very fast because there was no reliable way to transport it.

Then, in the 1850s, Springfield's founder, Elias Briggs, built the largest and most important early sawmill, and more mills opened in quick succession. Those early timber operations depended on a network of natural waterways and man-made chutes, flumes and roads. Once downed trees reached the river, crews of loggers called "river rats" herded them downstream for milling.

The arrival of the railroad opened the doors of commerce to the timber industry, the leader of which was Booth-Kelly Lumber Company. At its high point, the company produced more than 143 million board feet of timber per year. A later arrival was Weyerhaeuser Company, an operation that bought many mills to become one of the world's largest timber companies today.

Timber isn't the whole agriculture story in Lane County. Hops were an important crop until the 1930s, when the Depression and a mildew epidemic required farmers to till under their crops. Workers, including regular crews of Native Americans from the Warm Springs Reservation, flocked to the fields at harvest time, picking, drying and sending away hops to German-style breweries in Portland and Vancouver.

For more than 150 years, Lane County farmers have been putting their rich soil to work. This area was America's first producer of hazelnuts, and its flax made hardy cloth and linseed oil. Fruits, vegetables, grain, mint and grass seed have remained staple crops. Eighty years ago, the county's granges sponsored the first farmer's market in downtown Eugene, a tradition that continues at the same location today.

Left: A view of early-day river logging taken at the head Millrace leading from the Willamette to the Booth-Kelly sawmill in Springfield, early 1900s. *Courtesy Springfield Museum*

Right: C.L. Williams log drive crew, Dexter, circa 1885. The drive was for Pengra Brothers Saw Mill in Springfield. *Courtesy Patricia Williams Jacobson*

Above: Loggers with peaveys on logs in Hills Creek, circa 1895. Men are identified as Nick Morehouse, Chaz. Wallace, Clarence Eaton, Joe Hills, Nelse Skeels, Ray Hills, Chaz. Hills, Bill Eaton, Johnny Hills, Jack Reufro and Luge Hills. *Courtesy Springfield Museum*

Left: Steam donkey at work in the woods, circa 1895. *Courtesy Springfield Museum*

Above: Log mill and pond near Dexter, circa 1895. *Courtesy Springfield Museum*

Left: Threshing crew near Junction City, early 1900s. *Courtesy Lane County Historical Museum*

Working the Land

Right: Liles hop yard, probably located in the Junction City or Crow area, circa 1900. *Courtesy Lane County Historical Museum*

Above: Loggers Les Griffins and Henry Madison, 1900. *Courtesy Springfield Museum*

Left: Herbert W. Walker wood sawing crew, 1895. In the early days wood was delivered to homes in four-foot lengths. The homeowner then hired a wood sawing crew to saw the wood in the proper length to accommodate his stove. Pictured from left, Charley Davis, unidentified, Bertha Walker, Alie Male, Ralph Walker, Marion Davis, Fred Walker, and Finley Male. *Courtesy Springfield Museum*

Above: Horse logging in Lane County, 1903. *Courtesy Springfield Museum*

Right: LeSells Stewart atop a logjam on the Willamette River, circa 1900. *Courtesy Springfield Museum*

Above: Loggers at work with a downhill log skid, circa 1900. *Courtesy Springfield Museum*

Left: Logging train at Landax, early 1900s. *Courtesy Springfield Museum*

Working the Land

Above: Logging crew at the Montgomery Bros. Camp on the McKenzie River, circa 1904. *Courtesy Springfield Museum*

Above: Tree falling, Big Fall Creek, 1903. *Courtesy Springfield Museum*

Right: Apple harvesting at Watson's orchard in the Bailey Hill area, 1904. The women are believed to be members of the Conger family. *Courtesy Lane County Historical Museum*

Left: Harvesting grain on the Baxter Young farm near Fall Creek, circa 1905. Workers are using wooden cradles to separate grain from chaff. In the photo are Theodore Glaspy, Baxter Young, Roy Humphrey, Ruf Callison, Alie McClain, John McClain, Mark McClain, Jim Callison, George Renfrow and Geo. _____. *Courtesy Lane County Historical Museum*

Right: Women, children and men pick hops at the Irvin Barbee hop yard near Fall Creek, a community west of Lowell and north of the Willamette River, circa 1905. *Courtesy Lane County Historical Museum*

Above: Threshing crew poses with "Old Curley," an early tractor with steam engine and roof, at a farm just north of Eugene, circa 1906. *Courtesy Lane County Historical Museum*

Right: Threshing grain at Fred and Annie Wright's ranch near Walker, between Cottage Grove and Creswell, circa 1909. The steam tractor in the foreground, left, powers threshing machine at right via drive belt. Thresher blows chaff into tall straw stack at far right. Horse-drawn wagon waits by threshing machine with load of grain. The Wright ranch was established in 1891 and given Century Farm status in October 1990. *Courtesy Lane County Historical Museum*

Working the Land

Above: Logging crew members pose with steam donkey at site near Marcola, circa 1905. *Courtesy Lane County Historical Museum*

Left: Logging in the Wendling area, circa 1905. The man with the axe is J. Oliver Root. *Courtesy Katie Lytle*

Right: Logging in the Wendling area, circa 1905. The man at right is J. Oliver Root. *Courtesy Katie Lytle*

Left: Booth-Kelly Mill, Springfield, circa 1907. *Courtesy Springfield Museum*

Below: Booth-Kelly Lumber Co. crew, east of Springfield, early 1900s. Gilbert Simmons is identified as the fourth man from the right. *Courtesy Gladeus Simmons Pupke*

Above: Hills Brothers' Logging Company crew near Winberry, circa 1906. Crew members are identified as, left to right, standing, unknown, Oscar Trolson and Roy Hills. Seated, Charlie Hills, Fred Hills and John Cain. The No. 3 steam donkey was built for the Hills Brothers' Logging Company by Willamette Iron and Steel Company. *Courtesy Lane County Historical Museum*

Above: Harvesting peaches on the John Thramer farm on the Willamette River in what is now Eugene's Alton Baker Park, circa 1913. Included in the photo are Ruby Thramer, Allen Thramer, Forrest Blighton and Evelyn McKenney. *Courtesy Lane County Historical Museum*

Right: Group harvesting grain with horse-drawn threshing equipment near the community of Mohawk, north of Springfield, 1910. Threshing wheel in background; processing unit is on the right. *Courtesy Lane County Historical Museum*

Above: Steam donkey and crew yarding logs at Dietz Brothers Lumber Company in Eugene, circa 1910. *Courtesy Lane County Historical Museum*

Left: Logging crew poses on stacked lumber in front of flume, probably situated on Prune Hill, near Saginaw, circa 1910 *Courtesy Lane County Historical Museum*

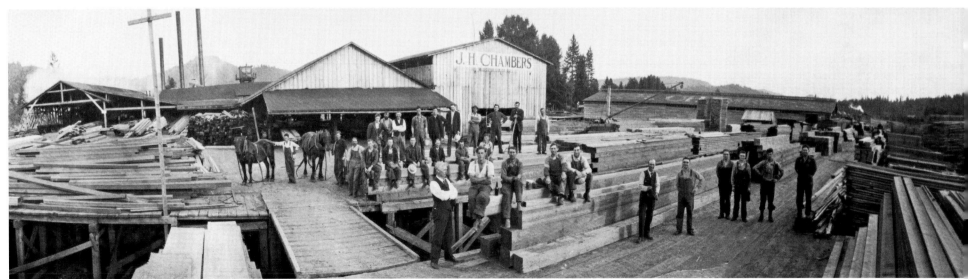

Above: Crew members pose with stacked wooden beams at Chambers Lumber Company sawmill, near Cottage Grove, circa 1910. *Courtesy Lane County Historical Museum*

Above: O.R. Sales hauls a load of wood to the Eugene Seltzer Mill from Springfield, South 2nd and D streets in Springfield, 1910. *Courtesy Donald P. Sales*

Above: Sidwell sisters and other workers at Seavey's hop yard, Springfield, September 15, 1910. *Courtesy Springfield Museum*

Right: Booth-Kelly logging locomotive with crew in tow, Wendling, circa 1910. *Courtesy Katie Lytle*

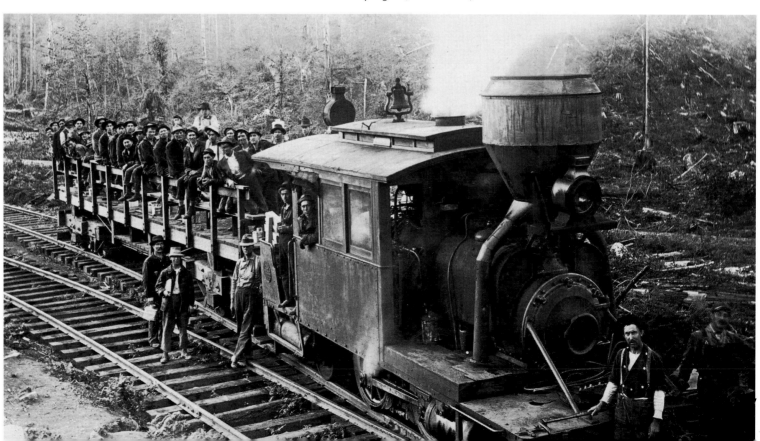

Left: Seavey's hop yard workers' encampment, Springfield, circa 1912. *Courtesy Springfield Museum*

Below: Seavey's hop yard workers pose for this photo, Springfield, circa 1914. *Courtesy Springfield Museum*

Above: Hops transported from the field in this horse-drawn, flatbed wagon in Springfield, circa 1914. *Courtesy Springfield Museum*

Above Right: Native American hop pickers at Seavey's hop yard, Springfield, circa 1914. *Courtesy Springfield Museum*

Right: Hop pickers work among the vine rows at James Seavey's hop yard and ranch on the McKenzie River north of Springfield and four miles east of the present-day I-5 freeway bridges, circa 1914. *Courtesy Lane County Historical Museum*

Above: "Stringers" at Seavey's hop yard, Springfield, circa 1914. *Courtesy Springfield Museum*

Right: Steam donkey with cable tower and three workers in the early 1900s.
Courtesy Springfield Museum

Below: Sidwell sisters at Seavey's hop yard, Springfield, 1914. *Courtesy Springfield Museum*

Above: Henry C. Cook's vegetable stall in Eugene's first Producer's Market on the northwest corner of 8th Avenue and Oak Street, circa 1917. *Courtesy Lane County Historical Museum*

Left: A young man holds a crate of freshly picked loganberries in a Lane County field, circa 1914. *Courtesy Lane County Historical Museum*

Above: Alfred Noble, left, and Oscar Noble, cutting down a large tree with a crosscut saw and springboards in the Armitage Park area, 1920s. *Courtesy Gary D. Noble*

Right: View of Eugene Fruit Growers Association plant, looking south on Ferry Street, circa 1920. *Courtesy Katie Lytle*

Above: Loaded grain trucks outside Springfield Mill and Grain Company, 1925. *Courtesy Springfield Museum*

Above: Workers at Anderson's hop house in Walterville pose for this photo, circa 1921.

Courtesy Springfield Museum

Right: Packing house at the Eugene Fruit Growers Association plant, circa 1920.

Courtesy Katie Lytle

Left: Forcey & Larson logging crew, circa 1936. The mill was between Walton and Noti. The only one identified is Everett Miller, first row, seventh from left.
Courtesy Becky Stringfield

Above: Everett Miller working on steam donkey for Forcey & Larson logging between Walton and Noti, circa 1936. *Courtesy Becky Stringfield*

Right: George and Lenora Jennings (couple on the right), were the owners of Lead Crystal Mines, 1930. This group is standing in front of a display advertising Western Oregon Mining Congress. *Courtesy Barbara Anheluk*

Above: Alfred Noble poses with a large log on a wooden trestle at Hult Lumber Company, 1939. *Courtesy Gary D. Noble*

Left: Hurd's hop field crew, Coburg, circa 1931. *Courtesy Fran Miller*

CHAPTER THREE

Transportation

Today, the automobile is king, but it didn't always rule Lane County roads. Before automobiles arrived in the early 1900s, the roads belonged to bicycles, horse-drawn carts and buggies, stage-coaches, trolleys and even mule-drawn streetcars.

In the first decade of the 20th century, the roads in Eugene, Springfield and other towns were still unpaved. Everywhere they went, travelers contended with dirt and mud. Travel was messy and, compared with modern standards, exceedingly slow. A trip from Eugene or Springfield to the coast, which takes slightly more than 1 hour by automobile today, lasted anywhere between three days and a week, by all accounts.

Stagecoach travel is responsible for establishing many of Lane County's outlying communities. Travelers and their horses needed to stop at regular intervals to sleep and give their horses rest.

Travel changed drastically with the arrival of a railroad line from Portland in 1871. Now, loggers and farmers could easily send their harvests to other parts of the country, and the county's economy began to flourish. Additionally, people could comfortably travel long distances. By 1915, five trains a day ran between Eugene and Portland.

The Willamette and McKenzie rivers were both too shallow to accommodate the kind of travel and transportation that the founders of Eugene and Springfield had envisioned. From a transportation stand-point, the rivers were often considered barriers between city dwellers and the fields they wanted to reach for work.

Pioneers who once forded rivers in their wagons must have been delighted by the new technology that allowed them to cross rivers using a sturdy cabled ferry system. One of the best-known crossing points was Deadmond Ferry, which transported many workers to and from fields on the north side of the McKenzie River.

Eugene's first automobile is said to have been the steam-powered rig purchased by the owner of Ax Billy department store in downtown Eugene. From there, cars and trucks proliferated each decade, growing far beyond their initial status as possessions of the rich and famous.

Left: Two members of the first round-the-world flying crew prepare to enter a limousine during a visit to Eugene, September 27, 1924. *Courtesy Lane County Historical Museum*

Right: Wiley Griffin poses with the mule-drawn streetcar that he drove from Willamette Street to the University of Oregon, circa 1893. The mule-driven line was owned by Henry W. Holden, and was later replaced by Portland, Eugene & Eastern Company's electric line. Wiley Griffin was one of Eugene's first African-American residents. *Courtesy Lane County Historical Museum*

Above: Horse-drawn buggy in front of the Thurston Post Office and Store, circa 1900. *Courtesy Springfield Museum*

Left: Floyd Frye goes for a ride in his horse-drawn buggy at 6th and North A streets, Springfield, early 1900s. *Courtesy Springfield Museum*

Above: Streetcars on Modoc Street, Springfield, early 1900s. *Courtesy Springfield Museum*

Right: Frank L. and Ida Chambers pose on a bicycle with their daughter, Mary, in front of their two-story Victorian home at 594 Lincoln Street, circa 1900. The house was on the northwest corner of 9th Avenue and Lincoln Street, and later moved to 1006 Taylor Street, on the southwest corner of 10th Avenue and Taylor. *Courtesy Lane County Historical Museum*

Right: The first street-car in Springfield, circa 1905. *Courtesy Springfield Museum*

Above: Construction of the Hendricks Bridge at Hendricks Ferry, circa 1907. *Courtesy Springfield Museum*

Left: McKenzie River stage at the post barn in Walterville, circa 1905. As driver Ed Walker and passenger Belle Sparks prepare to leave, a small boy watches at left. *Courtesy Lane County Historical Museum*

Opposite page: Early automobiles line 9th Avenue between Oak and Pearl streets, Eugene, on the occasion of overland race from New York to Seattle, circa 1909. *Courtesy Lane County Historical Museum*

Left: Southern Pacific Company railroad depot, Coburg, circa 1910. *Courtesy Lane County Historical Museum*

Above: Employees pose for the photo in the office of Southern Pacific Company's freight house at the north end of Charnelton Street, Eugene, circa 1910. Agent was A.J. Gillette, probably seated at the desk. *Courtesy Lane County Historical Museum*

Left: Southern Pacific Company section men pose on a pump car in front of a storage shed, June 14, 1910. Photographer, Smith Mountjoy, kneels at right and pulls camera cable. *Courtesy Lane County Historical Museum*

Above: Two crew members pose in the doorway of the Fairmount Boulevard streetcar of the Portland, Eugene & Eastern Company street railway line, circa 1910. *Courtesy Lane County Historical Museum*

Right: The Smith family in William Smith's new Cadillac, May 1912. Byron Smith is at the steering wheel. The auto is parked in front of the 1909 U.S. Post Office on the northwest corner of 5th Avenue and Willamette Street. *Courtesy Lane County Historical Museum*

Above: Steam locomotives at the Southern Pacific Railway depot, at the north end of Willamette Street, Eugene, circa 1911. *Courtesy Lane County Historical Museum*

Left: McKenzie River stage stop at Gate Creek, near Vida, circa 1910. The stage and horses are waiting in front of the home of Ben and Frank Minney, who, with their wives, operated a hotel and provided meals for travelers. The stage stop was discontinued in 1913 when automobiles became more common. *Courtesy Lane County Historical Museum*

Left: Pioneer Pageant visitors examine Mahlon Sweet's "White Gas Car," which traveled the roads of Lane County, circa 1913. The car is parked in the lot of Sweet-Drain Auto Company on the southwest corner of 10th Avenue and Oak Street. *Courtesy Lane County Historical Museum*

Above: Southern Pacific Railroad depot at 919 Main Street, Cottage Grove, circa 1915. *Courtesy Lane County Historical Museum*

Right: Smith Mountjoy in his car on the Deadmond Ferry, circa 1914. *Courtesy Springfield Museum*

Above: Wayne Yarnell gives his friends a ride in this fancy automobile in Eugene, circa 1917. *Courtesy Katie Lytle*

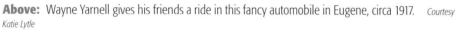

Left: Southern Pacific railroad tie plant at Cottage Grove, 1915. *Courtesy Lane County Historical Museum*

Above: Smith Mountjoy rides around town on his fancy motorcycle, Springfield, circa 1915. *Courtesy Springfield Museum*

Left: Ralph H. Pierce in his automobile in front of his garage in Eugene. He later invented the Pierce Coupler and started R.H. Pierce Manufacturing. *Courtesy Katie Lytle*

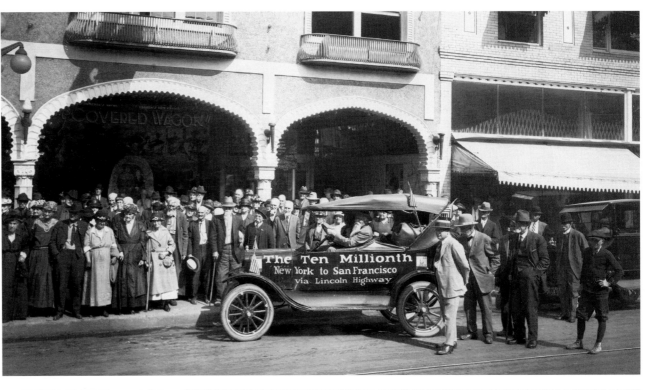

Above: Training room of Hobi Airways located on Road 3, west of Eugene city limits, Eugene Airfield, 18th and Chambers Street, October 22, 1928. *Courtesy Lane County Historical Museum*

Right: Townspeople gather to see the "Ten Millionth Car" which traveled from New York to San Francisco via Lincoln Highway. The gathering is in front of the Rex Theatre at 977 Willamette Street in Eugene, circa 1924. *Courtesy Lane County Historical Museum*

Above: Members of the first round-the-world flight team visit Eugene with their biplanes, September 27, 1924. *Courtesy Lane County Historical Museum*

Left: A goat cart was one way to get around Eugene, circa 1925. *Courtesy Lane County Historical Museum*

Above: The "Last Laugh," experimental aircraft invented by Roy Scroggs of Eugene, circa 1930. The wingless craft's design was based on the concept of a paper dart. It used less fuel and was said to be safer than conventional airplanes because of its gliding capacity.   *Courtesy Lane County Historical Museum*

Above: Three unidentified men pose with an automobile advertising Lane Auto Co. and Star Chassis, Eugene, circa 1925. Lane Auto Co. was at 834 Pearl Street.   *Courtesy Lane County Historical Museum*

Right: Grand opening of the Siuslaw River Bridge, Highway 101, Florence, March 31, 1936. The Hotel Florence is on the riverbank in the center of the photo, between the Hurd residence and public school.   *Courtesy Lane County Historical Museum*

CHAPTER FOUR

Commerce & Industry

Never have Lane County cities been on the scale of industrial giants like Detroit and Pittsburgh. From the beginning, this county's claim to fame has been its natural resources. Not surprisingly, lasting prosperity arrived when its lumber and other crops could reliably be transported to buyers throughout the world. Boat, train and truck - all have been parts of the area's economic lifeline.

In the early 1900s, semi-trucks weren't even a twinkle in an inventor's eye. Commerce depended on the train. Whole cities oriented themselves around train stations to make loading and unloading as easy as possible. Every day whistles downtown meant new goods for store shelves and more sales for lumbermen and farmers.

Today's shopper would hardly recognize the early establishments open for business. Meat shops didn't sport refrigerator cases filled with tidy cuts; they featured full carcasses and buckets of lard hanging from the ceiling. Dry goods shops were the predecessors of modern department stores. Residents made their own bread and canned their own fruits and vegetables. But by the 1920s they began depending more heavily on grocery stores and bakeries.

In the late 1800s, every large community had at least one flour mill to supply homemakers and bakeries. Side by side were sawmills and woolen mills. Most of these operations were located along the rivers or man-made canals crisscrossing the community. Vestiges of these millraces now serve boaters and local wildlife.

Blacksmith shops were as common as tire and oil-changing shops are in the 21st century. Residents depended on horses, and they depended on their local blacksmith for a good set of horseshoes. Blacksmiths were also regularly employed to repair pots, bridles and anything else made of metal. At the time, repair was exponentially cheaper than buying replacements.

Some things never change, even over a century. Newspapers in Eugene, Springfield and Junction City were covering all the news fit to print. Barbers, bankers, jewelers, restaurant owners and salesmen were meeting the same needs consumers have today.

Left: Employees of Rex Café pose behind the counter, circa 1936. The business was located at 92 West 8th Avenue in Eugene.   *Courtesy Lane County Historical Museum*

Right: Piper and Holderman's Hardware Store, the first in Cottage Grove, on the northwest corner of South River Road and Willamette Court, circa 1891.   *Courtesy Lane County Historical Museum*

Above: Office of the Junction City Bulletin, circa 1895. The only one identified is the woman, Mrs. Oglesby. *Courtesy Lane County Historical Museum*

Left: Interior of Fisher and Watkins Meat Market on the east side of Willamette Street between 7th and 8th avenues, Eugene, December 1895. Notice the tins of lard hanging from the ceiling. *Courtesy Lane County Historical Museum*

Right: Willamette Market (meat market), on the west side of Willamette Street between 7th and 8th avenues, 1893. Charles Walker Young and his son, Cal Young, owned this market; they are standing in front of the market on the far left. The man at the far right is Chris Bartsch. The others are unidentified. *Courtesy Lane County Historical Museum*

Above: Workers pose with pickaxes at rock quarry north of Cottage Grove, circa 1901. Two women, Minnie and Lillian Goodenow, stand to the right. The man in the center wearing a white shirt is identified as Will Goodenow. *Courtesy Lane County Historical Museum*

Left: S.H. Friendly Store at 594 Willamette Street (pre-1914 address), Eugene, circa 1894. The men are identified as Jesse Cohen, unidentified, T.J. Nicklin, S.H. Friendly and A.T. Cockerline. This store carried dry goods. *Courtesy Lane County Historical Museum*

Left: William Trimble's blacksmith shop, Eugene, circa 1900. *Courtesy Lane County Historical Museum*

Right: George Griffith at work in his Cottage Grove barber shop, early 1900s. *Courtesy Lane County Historical Museum*

Above: Henry and William C. Standley in their popcorn and peanut wagon, Eugene, circa 1911. *Courtesy Bray family*

Right: Littlefield's Cigar Store at 529 Willamette Street (pre-1914 address), between 8th and 9th avenues, Eugene, circa 1902. This business was owned by Charles F. Littlefield (pictured at left). His son, Ray, is pictured at right. *Courtesy Lane County Historical Museum*

Above: Cox & Cox clothing and dry goods store on the northwest corner of 5th and Main streets, Springfield, early 1900s. *Courtesy Springfield Museum*

Right: W.F. Walker, Springfield undertaker and his horse-drawn hearse in front of his business. *Courtesy Springfield Museum*

Above: Group photo in front of the pool hall on Main Street, Springfield, circa 1900. Pictured here are Wiley Humphries, Walter Burgess, Judy Burgess, Ed Burgess, Ronald Roberts, Joe Fry, John Ennis, Floyd Fry, Arnie Nelson, Earl Laxton, Dutch Walker, Jim McPherson, Cecil Wilmot, Fat McGill, Ed Dompier, and Johnny Sinnar. *Courtesy Springfield Museum*

Left: First National Bank of Eugene, northwest corner of Willamette Street and Broadway (9th Avenue), 1903. Identified in the photo, left to right are P.E. Snodgrass, cashier; S.S. Spencer; S.B. Eakin, vice-president; Frank McCallister; Lewis Potter; on stairway at entrance to vault, Charles Scott; in lobby, standing outside cages, President T.G. Hendricks; L.L. Goodrich; James H. Gilbert. *Courtesy Lane County Historical Museum*

Above: Employees of the J. Marsh Martin Brickyard located on West 11th Avenue, circa 1905. *Courtesy Lane County Historical Museum*

Right: Rathmell and Branstetter Barbershop at 506 Willamette Street (pre-1914 address), between 7th and 8th avenues, Eugene, circa 1908. The man on the right is identified as Will Branstetter, the man on the left as Rathmell and the customer, unknown. *Courtesy Lane County Historical Museum*

Above: Seventeen drays waiting in line on Willamette Street between 6th and 7th avenues in Eugene to unload pianos at Morris Piano Shop, October 17, 1906. *Courtesy Lane County Historical Museum*

Left: Creswell Creamery company employees are posing with milk cans in front of the business in Creswell, circa 1908. The delivery wagon waits at the curb. *Courtesy Lane County Historical Museum*

Commerce & Industry

Above: Eagle Cigar Store, on the northwest corner of Main and 7th streets. Clerk on the left is identified as Anchor Alstead; man on the right is believed to be Warren McFarland. *Courtesy Lane County Historical Museum*

Above: The Junction City Times office, circa 1910. Man on the left is Walter Jacobsen. Man in background with hat is Times owner, Steele L. Moorhead. *Courtesy Lane County Historical Museum*

Right: Schwarzschild's Book Store at 586 Willamette Street (pre-1914 address). Individuals are identified, left to right as Wallace Potter, Darrel Bristow, unidentified, Elsie Dirkheimer, unidentified woman and Morris Schwartzchild. *Courtesy Lane County Historical Museum*

Below: Employees of the J. Marsh Martin Brickyard located on West 11th Avenue, circa 1905. *Courtesy Lane County Historical Museum*

Above: Men's cigar store in Springfield was a gathering place for the local men to congregate, circa 1910. *Courtesy Springfield Museum*

Left: The Eugene Band and a large crowd in front of the Commercial Club Building on the northwest corner of Willamette Street and 10th Avenue, circa 1910. *Courtesy Lane County Historical Museum*

Above: Preston & Hales Harness Shop at 857 Willamette Street, Eugene, circa 1914. Man in foreground is identified as "Anderson." *Courtesy Lane County Historical Museum*

Left: Springfield flour mill, circa 1910. W.H. Stearmer is the only one identified. *Courtesy Springfield Museum*

Below: O. Peterson blacksmithing shop on the southwest corner of 5th and Greenwood streets, Junction City, circa 1914. *Courtesy Lane County Historical Museum*

Above: The Ford service garage in Springfield, circa 1920. *Courtesy Springfield Museum*

Left: Alec K. Patterson's Meat Market at 15 East 9th Avenue, Eugene, circa 1920. Alec Patterson is sitting with his grandson, Stu, behind him. The man with the mustache is Joe Brauner. Girdon Sumers is standing beside the cash register. *Courtesy Lane County Historical Museum*

Right: Salesmen pose with a truck carrying vacuum cleaners in front of the Eureka Vacuum Cleaner Company at 27 East 9th Avenue, Eugene, December 1925. *Courtesy Lane County Historical Museum*

Above: Insurance offices of Charles F. Littlefield and Ray H. Littlefield, Merchants Protective Association of Eugene at 504 Willamette (pre-1914 address), Eugene, 1911. *Courtesy Lane County Historical Museum*

Right: Eugene Broughton's jewelry store, on the north side of 6th Street, near Greenwood Street, Junction City, circa 1914. Charlie Barker poses near the exhibit cases. *Courtesy Lane County Historical Museum*

Above: A Chrysler Model 50 automobile in the window at McMorran & Washburne Department Store at 904 Willamette Street, Eugene, August 24, 1926. This photo was taken for Publix Motors at 929 Oak Street. *Courtesy Lane County Historical Museum*

Left: Preston and Hale's Fuller Paint Store at 857 Willamette Street, Eugene, circa 1925. *Courtesy Lane County Historical Museum*

Above: Morning Register at 119 East 9th Avenue, Eugene, circa 1927. Wetherbee-Powers Furniture Company was located in this building on the ground floor. *Courtesy Lane County Historical Museum*

Right: Employees posed in front of the F.W. Pettyjohn Motor Company at 63 West 7th Avenue, Eugene, June 19, 1926. *Courtesy Lane County Historical Museum*

Left: Hargreaves and Lindsay employees "Saving Eugene Streets," circa 1927. *Courtesy Lane County Historical Museum*

Right: This photo was taken where the University of Oregon Daily Emerald "put out" the Guard, circa 1927. The picture is in the alley next to the Guard building when it was at 1041 Willamette Street. In the photo, from left are, Bill Tugman, managing editor, A.F. Baker, the new publisher, Fred Guyon, city editor, Sid Jenkins of the Guard, Lyle Kelling, Guard advertising man, Bill Hagerty and Dick Godfrey of the Emerald staff. *Courtesy The Register-Guard*

Below: A.C. Mathews Sand and Gravel on East 8th Avenue, Eugene, circa 1925. *Courtesy Lane County Historical Museum*

Above: Midgley Planing Mill Co., Eugene, 1921. *In memory of Bob Schmieding, Don Schmieding and Duane Marshall, last owners before Eugene Water and Electric Board purchased this property at 4th and High Street*

Above: Eugene Water Board's hydroelectric power plant at Leaburg on the McKenzie River, June 8, 1929. The workmen are installing a generator. *Courtesy Lane County Historical Museum*

Left: Construction of Eugene Water Board's hydroelectric dam at Leaburg on the McKenzie River, August 17, 1928. The workmen are placing reinforcing steel on large pipes (the "penstock"). *Courtesy Lane County Historical Museum*

Above: The Rainbow Restaurant at 820 Willamette Street, Eugene, October 20, 1927. *Courtesy Lane County Historical Museum*

Above: Roney Brothers Store in Goshen, circa 1927. Anthony L. and L. Nelson Roney came to Dexter from Pennsylvania in the late 1800s. They bought this store in 1891 from J.W. Matlock. Raliegh Roney, son of Nelson, operated the store until about 1927 and sold it to a Mr. Phillips. Raliegh was the Goshen postmaster until his death in the 1930s. Pictured here, left to right are, Raliegh Roney, his wife Ruth Roney, and his father L. Nelson Roney. *Courtesy Springfield Museum*

Left: General Gasoline Station, Triangle Service Station on West 6th Avenue and Blair Boulevard, Eugene, January 9, 1928. *Courtesy Lane County Historical Museum*

SKAGGS UNITED STORES
ASH STORES
BUTTER MARGARINE 25¢ Pound
CRYSTAL WHITE SOAP 10 BARS 3
CORN MEAL 2 BAGS 65¢
GROCERIES
GROCERIES
PAN-DANDY BREAD

Above: Day-Nite Garage, owned by Otto Eidson and James H. Brown, late 1920s. It was at 645 Olive Street in Eugene. *Courtesy Mabel Eidson Rear*

Above: Eugene Packing Company located at the site where the present day Alton Baker Park is located, Eugene, April 13, 1928. *Courtesy Lane County Historical Museum*

Left: Employees pose in front of Skaggs grocery store at 95 West Broadway on the northeast corner of Broadway and Olive Street, Eugene, circa 1928. *Courtesy Lane County Historical Museum*

Right: Employees of *The Eugene Guard* and the newly installed press, May 18, 1928. The newspaper office was at 1037 Willamette Street. *Courtesy Lane County Historical Museum*

Above: Interior of the ice cream parlor in Wendling, owned by the Prouse family, circa 1930. Behind the counter are Ruth and Grover Wilson. Seated in front of the counter is Mr. Godfrey and at the table is Mrs. Wilson, Grover's mother. *Courtesy Springfield Museum*

Above: Interior of Buster Brown Shoe Store at 933 Willamette Street, Eugene, March 3, 1928. *Courtesy Lane County Historical Museum*

Left: Delivery cars and employees line up in front of Hillis & Mogan Office Equipment at 31 East 7th Avenue, Eugene, circa 1930. *Courtesy Lane County Historical Museum*

Right: Rose Bud Bakery at 82 West Broadway Avenue, Eugene, September 12, 1931. *Courtesy Lane County Historical Museum*

Above: A large crowd attends an auction at Hoffman Jewelry on Willamette Street in Eugene, November 12, 1932. *Courtesy Lane County Historical Museum*

Above: Window display at McMorran & Washburne Department Store, 904 Willamette Street, Eugene, October 19, 1931. *Courtesy Lane County Historical Museum*

Left: Uniformed staff members of Pay 'n Takit Market pose with the Heinz Ketchup display. The market was at 101 East Broadway Street in Eugene, January 20, 1932. *Courtesy Lane County Historical Museum*

Right: A crowd gathers in front of The Leader for a big sale. The Leader was a women's apparel and dry goods store at 860 Willamette Street in Eugene, November 30, 1932. *Courtesy Lane County Historical Museum*

Below: Interior of Bray's Grocery, Eugene, 1930. *Courtesy Bray family*

Above: Women and girls in a long admission line at an event in the Heilig Theatre at 676 Willamette Street in Eugene, September 1, 1934. *Courtesy Lane County Historical Museum*

Right: Interior of Groceteria at 94 West Broadway, Eugene, circa 1934. Staff members pictured, left to right are, George Orr, Lee Orr, Ted Bush (behind meat counter), and Cliff Pruett at produce scales. *Courtesy Lane County Historical Museum*

Left: Employees attend to their baking inside the Rose Bud Bakery at 82 West Broadway, Eugene, December 26, 1933. *Courtesy Lane County Historical Museum*

Right: Interior view of the Eugene Foundry and Machine Company, 518 East 8th Avenue, Eugene, circa 1934. *Courtesy Lane County Historical Museum*

Above: Montgomery Ward & Co. at 1059-1071 Willamette Street, Eugene, December 21, 1934. *Courtesy Lane County Historical Museum*

Left: Interior of Safeway, Eugene, circa 1935. At the time of this photo, Safeway had two stores, one at 109 East Broadway and 95 West Broadway. It is not known which location this photo was taken. *Courtesy Lane County Historical Museum*

Above: E. Burr Miller, manager of the first Safeway store in Eugene at the corner of Oak and Broadway, circa 1933. *Courtesy Nancy Nelson*

Right: Safeway Store at 109 East Broadway, Eugene, August 7, 1935. *Courtesy Lane County Historical Museum*

Above: Skeie's Jewelry at 927 Willamette Street, Eugene, circa 1935. Mr. Skeie is behind the counter at left. *Courtesy Lane County Historical Museum*

Above right: University of Oregon's NCAA basketball championship window display at the Rose Bud Bakery, April 1, 1939. The players are made out of bread loaves sitting on a bench. Pictured from left are Wally Johansen (#32), John Dick (#18), Laddie Gale (#28), Bobby Anet (#20) and "Slim" Wintermute. *Courtesy Lane County Historical Museum*

Right: Standard Station, 211 East Broadway, Eugene, circa 1939. *Courtesy Lane County Historical Museum*

Above: August F. "Gus" Bremer sits at station — "Machine No 1" — at The Register-Guard. Alton F. Baker, publisher of the newspaper from 1927-1961, looks on. Bremer worked at this spot more than 30 years, starting in 1911.

Above left: Rose Bud Bakery at 56 West Broadway, Eugene, 1937. *Courtesy Lane County Historical Museum*

Left: Rex Theatre at 969 Willamette Street, Eugene, circa 1939. *Courtesy Lane County Historical Museum*

CHAPTER FIVE

Schools & Education

The biggest - and often overlooked - difference between education past and present is the fact that our ancestors weren't always required to go to school. All states in the U.S. didn't compel all children to attend elementary school until 1918. Nationally only one-third of high school-age students took classes in the 1920s.

In Lane County, however, education was important to residents from the get-go. Proponents were dreaming of founding a university when Eugene and Springfield were scarcely platted.

First, though, came the elementary schools. Eugene and Springfield opened schools almost simultaneously in the 1850s. Springfield students were under the tutelage of a prim young Scottish woman named Agnes Stewart. Eugene students attended a tax-funded school on the corner of 11th Avenue and Olive Street. By 1876, the Eugene school had more than 400 students; Springfield reported 120 students in 1891.

High school students were the first to split away from these all-in-one schools. New schools with specialized curriculum for older students popped up everywhere. By 1940, nearly 75 percent of high school-age students were attending classes nationwide.

In old school photographs, students are sometimes cheerful but often solemn as they pose in athletic uniforms, band outfits, gradu-

ation finery or everyday clothes. Familiar music instruments and athletic equipment is present, but much is alien to modern students. Girls on Junction City High School's basketball team in 1910 played in dresses and only ran half the court. In 1935, 32 proud young men turned out for a picture of Eugene High School's boxing team. Today, none of the county's high schools sanction this pugilistic sport.

The first post-high school institution in Lane County was Columbia College, built in 1856 by Cumberland Presbyterian Church on what is now College Hill in south Eugene. Only days after classes began, the building burned. It was rebuilt, only to be destroyed by fire again a year later. The University of Oregon opened in 1876 as a tuition-free institution. It was followed in 1895 by the Eugene School of Divinity (now Northwest Christian College) and in 1925 by the Bible Standard Theological School (now Eugene Bible College).

Left: Hopkins school students and faculty pose on the steps of their school in Eugene, circa 1895. *Courtesy Lane County Historical Museum*

Right: Classroom of Eugene Business College, circa 1905. *Courtesy Lane County Historical Museum*

Above: Students pose on the steps of Dexter School, circa 1892. *Courtesy Lane County Historical Museum*

Left: Geary School students pose for the photographer, circa 1890. The school was on the north side of 4th Avenue between Madison and Monroe streets (later 751 West 4th Avenue), Eugene. *Courtesy Lane County Historical Museum*

Right: Eugene High School boys basketball team, 1906-07. Student in the right foreground is Robert Benson Kuykendall, University of Oregon, class of 1913. Young man in foreground, left, is Harold Cockerline, University of Oregon class of 1912. *Courtesy Lane County Historical Museum*

Right: Geary School's fourth grade class, circa 1907. *Courtesy Lane County Historical Museum*

Below: Students pose in front of Pleasant Hill School, 1906. Pictured, back row are the teacher, H.E. Inlow, Charles Sherwood, Lloyd Wiltse, Lee Davis, and Lou Furrow. Third row, Burns Renwick, Jeanie West, Althea Statzer, Hilda Miller, Ada Statzer, Eva Skaggs, and Pearl Higgins. Second row, Court Lattin, Jesse Furrow, Dudley Taylor, Mark Latten, Paul Taylor, Roy Renwick, Arlo Bristow, Grant Lattin, Prentice Callison, Edward Miller, and George Sherwood. First row, Pete Weaver, Lucille Callison, Clara Statzer, Lizzie West, Ida Schermer, Iris Statzer, Ruth Davis, Dorothy Taylor, Marie Sherwood, Sol Taylor, and Carl Weaver. *Courtesy Lane County Historical Museum*

Above: Harrisburg 8th grade graduating class, 1907. Included in the photo are John Harold, Edna Annis, Chester Riggs, Everett Garstam, Georgia Woods, Silas Gilbertson, Leona Anderson, Myrtle Gooding, Clarence Grimes, Smith Mountjoy, Miss Hughes, Ruby Scott, Lee Mountjoy, and Eva McLain. *Courtesy Springfield Museum*

Schools & Education

Above: Eugene High School class-room, circa 1908. The high school was on the southwest corner of 11th Avenue and Willamette Street until 1915. *Courtesy Lane County Historical Museum*

Above left: Eugene Divinity School classroom, circa 1907. *Courtesy Northwest Christian College Archives*

Left: Eugene High School football team, circa 1908. *Courtesy Lane County Historical Museum*

Left: Eugene High School on the southwest corner of Willamette Street and 11th Avenue, Eugene, circa 1912. Central School can be seen in the background. *Courtesy Lane County Historical Museum*

Above: Coburg graduation class, 1908. Pictured, left to right, back row, James Bettis, Chet Taylor, Gilbert Simmons, Lynn and Loren Smith. Middle row, Erma Drury, Grace Wilkins, Anna Nelson and Beulah Ditto. Front row, Mable Clothes, Mrs. Jennifer Beaman (teacher), and Vera Cooper. *Courtesy Gladeus Simmons Pupke*

Right: Junction City High School girls basketball team, 1910. Team members are, Mae Clemo, Anna McFarland, Helen Lang Pelman, Louise Flint, Coralee Snell, Ruth Tomar (Milliorn) and Ethel Kirk. *Courtesy Lane County Historical Museum*

Above: Six members of the Cottage Grove High School girls basketball team pose with their coach, circa 1912. *Courtesy Lane County Historical Museum*

Right: Cottage Grove grade school classroom, circa 1912. The school was located on what became the corner of 2nd and Adam streets. *Courtesy Lane County Historical Museum*

Right: Springfield High School freshman class, 1921. Pictured left to right, first row, Ralph Cline, Kenneth Dillard, Verl Feagles, Jack Webb, Frank Rennie, Linn Endicott, Merl McMullin, Randolph Allen, Roy Schaeufer, Teddy Kinan, Vera Root, Iva Day, and Helen Eyler. Second row, Cecil Herbert, Belvin Doan, Loran Edmiston, Lenabelle Harper, Dessie Starks, Julia Godman, Bernice Jacobson, Gladys Hastings, Lucile Male, Johnny Tomseth, John Halsey, Harold Stewart, and Alice Ramsdall. Third row, Professor Roth, Zelma Abun, Alice Tomseth, Charlotte Stewart, Virgil McPherson, Eugene Gale, Audry McPherson, Herbert Taylor, Jay Grant, Bessie Winters, Lyn Bowman, and Clair Cheshire. Fourth row, Lucile Fritz, Beulah Thermon, Gladys Bauer, Viola Nelson, Myrtle Hauton, Florence Kaiser, Erma Herman, Aliene Collier, and Gerald Endicot. Fifth row, Esther Fox, Lenore Dillard, Ada Carr, Lois Meats, Charline Lambert, and Adelaide Griel. Sixth row, Astrid Soleim, Myrtle Simms, Anna Dillard, Jennie Holverson, Mary Whitney, and Abbie Cooley. *Courtesy Katie Lytle*

Below: Campus of Eugene Bible University, Eugene, December 1, 1923. *Courtesy Northwest Christian College Archives*

Above: Brattain School 5th grade class, 1927. Pictured left to right, first row, Mary Smitson, Vivian Runte, Juanita Seamans, Donald Nelson, Faye Stratton, Echo Tomseth, Pearl Williams, and Elsie Beals. Second row, Lela Peterson, Clair Hadley, Martha Moon, Verlin Pasey, Aileen Clingenput, Dick Wright, Mae Pickell, _____ Hickman, and Ellen Cox. Third row, Bruce Squires, Ludie Godsey, Glen Wetzell, Mary Uchytil, Irvin House, and Francis Walker. *Courtesy Springfield Museum*

Above: Students in front of Geary School in Eugene, circa 1920. *Courtesy Donald P. Sales*

Right: Eugene High School baseball team of 1927. *Courtesy Lane County Historical Museum*

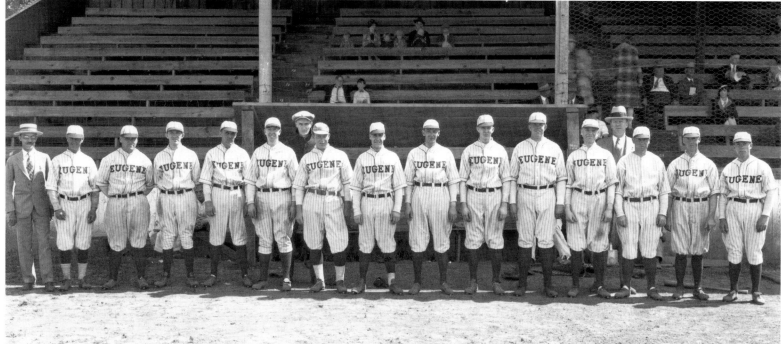

Right: Eugene Bible College preachers, circa 1932. Pictured left to right, Dr. S. Earl Childers, Walter L. Myers, Elmer Patterson, Allan Eiverson, Ira Bailes, Donald Ralston, Francis Beck, Paul Moore, William McLean, and Harry Benton. *Courtesy Northwest Christian College Archives*

Above: Santa Clara High School graduating class, June 1, 1929. *Courtesy Lane County Historical Museum*

Left: Eugene High School football team, December 5, 1930. *Courtesy Lane County Historical Museum*

Above: Eugene High School boxers, circa 1935.   *Courtesy Lane County Historical Museum*

Left: Northwest Christian College men's quartet, 1935. In the photo are Edward Dyer, Arthur Watters, Tingley Champie and Gerald Childers. *Courtesy Northwest Christian College Archives*

Above: Eugene High School dance, February 22, 1935. *Courtesy Lane County Historical Museum*

Right: Willagillespie School band poses in front of the school, Eugene, 1930s. The principal was Kenneth Kinzle. The school still stands today. *Courtesy Leo Gaskill*

Schools & Education

Above: Ruth Richardson's fourth grade class poses outdoor at Lincoln School, Eugene, circa 1939. The school was at 970 Monroe Street on the northwest corner of 10th Avenue and Monroe Street. *Courtesy Lane County Historical Museum*

Above: Coburg High School girls basketball team, 1938. Left to right, bottom row, Helen Thomason, Lillian Gray, _____Moser, Lucille Jones, Beatrice Bagwell, Jean Pitkin, and Carol Smith. Top row, Goldie McKinney, Ruth White, Gladeus Simmons, Shirley Smith, Helen Drury, and Claudia Smith. *Courtesy Gladeus Simmons Pupke*

Left: Springfield High School band members, 1938. Pictured left to right, front row, Gloria Green, Bruce Maxey, Raymond Dawson, Jim Stam, Barbra Rodgers, Donald Copenhaver, Bob Nice, Bob Stoddard, Frank Stewart, and Dana Austin. Back row, Frances Acheson, George Warner, Bob Strand, Carl Dittemore, Harold Wheeler, Lawrence Thompson, Lloyd Smith, Jane Phair, Ralph Warner, Paul Nott, Beryl Robertson, and Director Alvin Templer. *Courtesy Springfield Museum*

CHAPTER SIX
University Life

In 1876, who knew the fledgling University of Oregon - consisting of one building, five teachers and 177 students - would grow by the 21st century into a sprawling campus serving more than 20,000 students?

Early Lane County settlers knew they wanted a state university in Eugene. The town had lost its bid for state capital status to Salem, so its citizens were somewhat mollified by the Oregon legislature's decision to establish a state university in Eugene.

Raising funds for the new university was no easy task. Cash was scarce in the early 1870s, so supporters went door to door, visiting Eugene's 200 households and securing donations of labor and farm products. One founder, Judge J.J. Walton, was famous for convincing residents to donate a few chickens, a pig or a sack of grain to fund construction of the first UO building.

That building was Deady Hall, and it was barely finished in time for the first class. Those first students adhered to a strict code of conduct. They couldn't visit skating rinks or theaters. Drinking, dancing and profanity were prohibited. A thrilling social event of the day was the "walk-around," where male and female students spent an evening walking in pairs and quietly conversing.

Even before the first class graduated, a campus baseball club was forming. However, the team was disbanded after inebriated brawlers marred a game with Albany Collegiate Institute, which later became Lewis and Clark College. Football came next. The UO's first official football game was played in 1894 on a field next to Deady and Villard halls. Oregon beat the team from Albany, 44-2.

From its beginning, the UO was a source of entertainment and culture for Lane County residents. In addition to sporting events, townspeople turned out to observe rousing debates and musical events. Later, community theaters and choirs depended on the expertise of talented university staff. The bond between town and gown has only strengthened over the years.

Left: Opening day of the University of Oregon in October 1876. The building, Deady Hall, was just barely made habitable in time for the deadline set by the Oregon legislature. *Courtesy University of Oregon Special Collections*

Right: This scene is identified as the first University of Oregon football game, which was played in 1894 against Albany College (now Lewis & Clark College). UO won the game 44-2. The photograph is taken from the west side of campus near where Kincaid Street runs today, looking east. On the left is Villard Hall and in the center is Deady Hall. On the right is Friendly Hall, which was completed in 1893. Beyond Deady Hall can be seen the Gymnasium with its cupola. Built in 1890, it burned in 1922. *Courtesy University of Oregon Special Collections*

Above: University of Oregon students pose for a formal portrait in 1882. *Courtesy University of Oregon Special Collections*

Left: University of Oregon class of 1879. *Courtesy University of Oregon Special Collections*

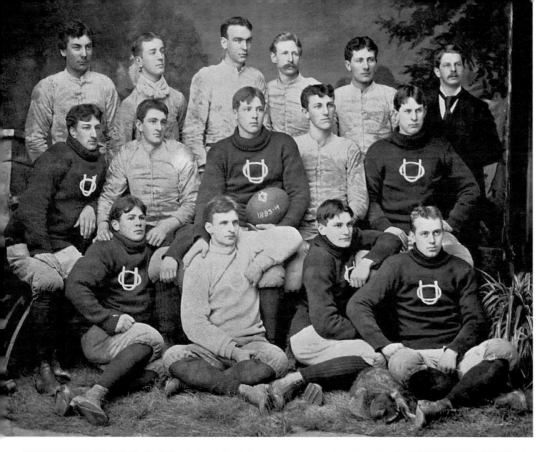

Above: The 1900 University of Oregon Women's Basketball Team. From left, back row, Vestella Sears, Lisa Straub, Mr. Charles A. Burden (Director of Physical Education), Ellizabeth Hackney, Elsie Perkins. Front row, Hattie Taylor, Salu (?) Holmes. *Courtesy University of Oregon Special Collections*

Above left: The first University of Oregon football team, circa 1894. *Courtesy University of Oregon Special Collections*

Left: The astronomical observatory was built in 1889 atop Skinner Butte by W. H. Abrams who constructed many buildings in Eugene. The building cost the university $4,782.78. Subject to vandalism and distant from the main campus, the building was abandoned by June 1898. On May 12, 1905, the observatory was demolished. *Courtesy University of Oregon Special Collections*

Left: Sam Friendly became a Regent of the University in 1895 and served on the Board of Regents for the next twenty years. He was instrumental in the growth of the University and active in its affairs. Friendly Hall was named for Sam Friendly. *Courtesy University of Oregon Special Collections*

Right: Luella Clay Carson held the chair of Rhetoric and Public Speaking from 1888 to 1895, Rhetoric and English Literature from 1903 to 1909, and was the first dean of women at the University of Oregon, serving in that capacity from 1895 to 1909. *Courtesy University of Oregon Special Collections*

Above: Construction of Gerlinger Hall in 1919. In 1929, the building was named for Irene H. Gerlinger, the first woman Regent, an avid fund-raiser and advocate for the University of Oregon. *Courtesy University of Oregon Special Collections*

Above: McClure Hall opened in 1900. It was named for Edgar McClure, a UO graduate who returned to the University to teach chemistry, and died climbing Mt. Rainier in 1897. For years, this building housed Chemistry among its other uses. In the 1920s, Lawrence's Journalism Building was attached to its west facade. McClure was demolished in 1953 to make way for the new Allen Hall. *Courtesy University of Oregon Special Collections*

Left: An early view of Deady Hall and Villard Hall. Villard Hall (right) was the second building on campus. It opened in 1886. *Courtesy University of Oregon Special Collections*

Above: The old Oregon Hall, circa 1925. *Courtesy University of Oregon Special Collections*

Above: University of Oregon football player and coach "Shy" Huntington, poses for a photo in front of the men's gym, circa 1920. Quarterback Charles "Shy" Huntington played football for UO from 1914 to 1916, was a key player in the 1917 Rose Bowl, and coached for UO from 1918 to 1923. He also coached the UO baseball team from 1919 to 1920. His football team went to the 1920 Rose Bowl, losing by only one point to Harvard. He resigned at the end of the 1923 season, saying "Each year my teams have been with me but the alumni have not...they have demanded a high-priced coach, a Bezdek or Dobie..." "Shy" was an All-American in 1916. He and his brother Hollis were inducted into the Rose Bowl Hall of Fame in 1992. *Courtesy University of Oregon Special Collections*

Left: Commencement exercises in 1921. *Courtesy University of Oregon Special Collections*

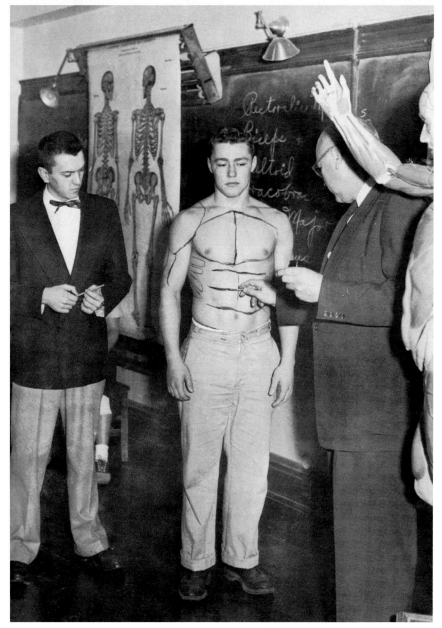

Above: Students working in a science laboratory at the university in 1935. *Courtesy University of Oregon Special Collections*

Right: This photo of a concert at McArthur Court provides a good view of the interior of the structure which was built in 1926. ASUO funded McArthur Court, named for Clifton N. 'Pat' McArthur, the first president of the ASUO (1899-1900), first editor of the student newspaper, and student director of athletics (1899-1900), member (and speaker) of the Oregon legislature and US Congress representative. Initially designed to seat 6,000, the arena was nicknamed the Igloo or Mac Court. *Courtesy University of Oregon Special Collections*

Above: Anatomy class at University of Oregon. *Courtesy University of Oregon Special Collections*

Right: Construction of the Physical Education building was completed in December 1936. This was a PWA project and at the entrance are two cast stone urns by PWA artist Walter Pritchard. The P. E. Building was later joined to the enclosed Leighton Pool and nearby McArthur Court. *Courtesy University of Oregon Special Collections*

Above: Presentation of the 1939 NCAA basketball trophy to Bobby Anet, team captain of the University of Oregon's men's basketball team, the "Tall Firs." Anet is standing on the right, accepting the trophy from Commissioner John Griffith, at left. Griffith was the first commissioner of the Western Intercollegiate Conference (now known as the Big Ten Conference). The athlete standing in the center has been identified as Jimmy Hull, of Ohio State University, and is receiving his trophy for the most outstanding player of the final four. *Courtesy University of Oregon Special Collections*

Above: Pep rally for the University of Oregon's men's basketball team, the "Tall Firs," in a packed arena in 1939. *Courtesy University of Oregon Special Collections*

Right: The Tall Firs receive an award. The three men on the left side of the image have been identified, from left to right, as John Dick, Laddie Gale, and Wally Johansen. The three men on the right side of the image have been identified, from left to right, as Bobby Anet (team captain), Slim Wintermute, and Coach Howard Hobson. *Courtesy University of Oregon Special Collections*

Opposite page: A large crowd gathers at the Eugene railroad station for the homecoming welcome for the University of Oregon's men's basketball team of 1938/39, the Tall Firs, after their championship victory in which they beat Ohio State 46-33, and won the first NCAA basketball championship title. *Courtesy University of Oregon Special Collections*

CHAPTER SEVEN

Community

The pioneer spirit was strong in Lane County's early residents, but it didn't keep them from coming together in work and play.

These fiercely independent people needed each other for some of life's most basic tasks. They helped each other build homes and barns. They weathered floods together. They pooled time and resources to start schools. They enforced laws and fought fires. In the early days, volunteerism was simply an ingredient for survival.

As in other American communities, families were much larger than today, and church attendance was practically a given. Immediately after settling in this area, pioneers established religious congregations. Starting with First Baptist Church in 1852, Eugene's first churches included Cumberland Presbyterian, St. Mary's Episcopal and First Methodist. Springfield's Baptist Church, built in 1871, and Eugene's First Christian Church, raised in 1911, are still standing, but most church buildings were destroyed long ago.

For entertainment, the community had to depend on itself at first. Music was a favorite; one family opened a music academy in the 1870s. The area's first performance centers were opera halls where audiences could attend operas, plays, musicals and vaudeville presented by touring companies. Many of these halls became movie theaters in the 1930s, but live performances remained popular.

When a man, woman or child needed medical attention, they generally depended upon traveling doctors. In the early 1900s, Springfield Private Hospital opened on Main Street. Then, not long after the end of World War I, the Eugene Hospital and Clinic opened.

In outlying areas, life was largely shaped by the harvest. Lumber companies built now-extinct communities — such as Star Camp, west of Veneta, and Wendling, east of Marcola — to house loggers and their families. In early fall, local hop fields swelled into temporary tent villages as entire families turned out to harvest the lucrative crop. These communities hosted dances, musical presentations and hundreds of memories for Lane County residents.

Left: Eugene Firemen's Band, circa 1910.   *Courtesy Lane County Historical Museum*

Right: Junction City Junior League members, 1898.
Courtesy Lane County Historical Museum

Above: Charles Edgar McClane, Eugene, late 1800s. *Courtesy Norma Roberts*

Right: John Henry McClane, five years old, was born in Oakridge. Photo, 1885. *Courtesy Norma Roberts*

Above: Members of Eugene Fire Department Hook and Ladder Company No. 1 pose on board sidewalk in front of City Hall on the north side of 8th Avenue between Oak and Willamette streets, circa 1890. *Courtesy Lane County Historical Museum*

Left: Springfield Coronet Band, circa 1880. Included in the band are Edd Newton, H. E. Walker, E. C. Martin, Alfred Wheeler, T. C. Wheeler, O. A. Wheeler, Ed Howe, Ed Poil, Chas. Neet and Ed Pengra. *Courtesy Springfield Museum*

Above: Alberta Shelton (later McMurphey), poses with a bicycle announcing her as being Eugene's "first lady-cyclist." Shelton was the daughter of Thomas W. Shelton who built the Shelton-McMurphey House at the north end of Willamette Street on the slopes of Skinner Butte. *Courtesy Lane County Historical Museum*

Above left: Mahlon Harlow and Frances Tandy Harlow, parents of Amelia Harlow Day, late 1800s. *Courtesy Springfield Museum*

Left: Eugene Volunteer Fire Department, Rescue Hose Team No. 3, circa 1895. From left, kneeling, Orange Callison, Frank Poindexter, Johnie Hess, Bert Jennings, and Roy Calloway. Standing, Will H. Hodes, John Dixon, Gardie Morris, Jim Billmire, Walter Hodes, and Bill Billmire. Frances Orton, child mascot, sits on the float in the background. *Courtesy Lane County Historical Museum*

Above: Mark Palmroy McClane and wife Ivy Grace Castleman, Eugene, late 1800s. *Courtesy Norma Roberts*

Right: Almanza Cameron McClane, Eugene, late 1800s. *Courtesy Norma Roberts*

Above: Members of the Eugene Fire Department pose for this photo, circa 1890. The man at left is identified as Charles E. Hollenbeck, brother of Florence Hollenbeck Jenkins. *Courtesy Lane County Historical Museum*

Left: Mahlon and Frances Harlow's 50th wedding anniversary, August 1885. Family members included are, Anderson Jackson Harlow, Henry Clay Harlow, Adelia Snelling Harlow, Sarah Naomi Harlow, Micajah B. Harlow, Judah Johanna Harlow, Margaret Ann Harlow, Jemima Frances Harlow, Mahlon Hall Harlow, Jr., Frances Burris Tandy Harlow, and Mahlon Hall Harlow. *Courtesy Marie Marshall*

Right: Amanda Gardner Johnson, Oregon pioneer of 1853. She was a slave girl belonging to the Anderson Deckard family. She was given her freedom when the family left for Oregon, but asked to come with them. The Deckards settled in Oakville in Linn County. Amanda postponed her marriage to blacksmith Ben Johnson (also a former slave) for five years while she cared for the motherless children of her former mistress, Elizabeth Deckard Snodgrass. One of the children was Pliny E. Snodgrass, president of the First National Bank of Eugene from 1917-1928. She was known as "Auntie Johnson" and lived in Albany until age 93. *Courtesy Lane County Historical Museum*

Above: M.M. Hill, a young African-American sailor, poses in uniform in Eugene. *Courtesy Lane County Historical Museum*

Left: The Rowe house at the corner of 1st and Monroe, Eugene, circa 1900. This home was built for Civil War veteran Alden Rowe by his sons in the late 1800s. Included in the photo are Fred Rowe, Emily Rowe, Elmer Kensler, Tom Kensler, Hattie Kensler (in chair), Eva Small, Virgil Small, Laura _____, Jonnie _____, Emma Sales, Orley Sales, Vesta Rowe, and Alden Rowe. *Courtesy Donald P. Sales*

Right: Children of Aaron Stanley and Clara Thomson, Junction City, circa 1895. Pictured, back row is baby Hattie and Stanford. In the front row is Ernest and Eva. *Courtesy Nancy Perkins Stiennon*

Above: Execution of Claude Branton on May 12, 1899 for the murder of John A. Linn at Isham's Corral in the McKenzie Pass. Branton was executed outside the Lane County Jail, on the northwest corner of 8th Avenue and Oak Street. Scene shows men on scaffold platform looking at trapdoor through which Branton's body has just dropped; man beneath scaffold is presumably holding the body. Branton, hired to help J.A. Linn herd livestock over the McKenzie Pass to the Willamette Valley, murdered Linn for money to marry a valley girl. Branton was tried and convicted at the Lane County Courthouse in Eugene. *Courtesy Lane County Historical Museum*

Left: The Liles family pose in front of their residence near the town of Crow, 1900. Pictured, from left to right are, Richard, Lucy, Katie, Virgil Liles and their two dogs. *Courtesy Lane County Historical Museum*

Right: Six boys pose for a photograph in Wendling, circa 1901. *Courtesy Lane County Historical Museum*

Above: A gathering around a trapped bear near Old Hill Road, Marcola, circa 1903. The bear was trapped by George Yarnall. Included in the photo are Mary Root Boggs, Alice Root Mathews (with gun), Harry Yarnall, Frank Root, John Austin Root, Jasper Evans, Ellen Josephine Root, Catherine "Cassie" Root Baxter, and John Oliver Root. *Courtesy Katie Lytle*

Right: A west Springfield family ready for a trip to the beach, circa 1903. It took a week to travel by wagon to the coast. Notice the two women wearing black bloomers. This was considered vulgar at the time of this photo. *Courtesy Springfield Museum*

Above: Eugene fire department, circa 1908. In 1905, the fire department finally got a pair of horses, Pete and Jerry. They were kept in a stall at the back of the fire station. When the alarm rang, firefighters would release a rope, automatically dropping harnesses onto the horses. *Courtesy Bray family*

Left: Eugene Fire Department fire wagon with driver, Charlie Croner, and horse team, Jerry and Pete, circa 1907. *Courtesy Lane County Historical Museum*

Below: Company "E" 4th Infantry band on a muddy West Main Street at the junction with H Street, Cottage Grove, circa 1907. Albert Woodward carries the bass drum; Ernest Leabo holds french horn to the left of Woodward. Hemenway Building on far left became the Masonic Hall when a second story was added later. It housed the National Guard headquarters in its basement. *Courtesy Lane County Historical Museum*

Left: Interior of the Springfield Post Office at 2nd and Main streets, early 1900s. *Courtesy Springfield Museum*

Right: Glenn Holt and mail wagon, Harrisburg, February 15, 1909. *Courtesy Springfield Museum*

Above: Christina Bertelsen family and their farm at the corner of Elmira and Bertelsen Road, Eugene, 1908. *Courtesy Barbara Harmon Bertelsen*

Left: Springfield Private Hospital, the city's first hospital, circa 1910. *Courtesy Springfield Museum*

Right: Alex Lundberg, owner of one of the freight lines that ran between Disston and Bohemia Mines. Lundberg was also the postmaster for the Bohemia Mines. *Courtesy Austin M. Pitcher*

Below: Henry Combs and his family pose in front of his residence on the Coast Fork of the Willamette River, between London and Black Butte, south of Cottage Grove, circa 1910. *Courtesy Lane County Historical Museum*

Above: Alex Lundberg House at the Musick Mine of the Bohemia Mines, circa 1910. The mine was located east of Cottage Grove. *Courtesy Austin M. Pitcher*

Left: Mrs. Zook's Coburg Methodist Church Sunday School class, circa 1910. Pictured left to right, first row, Gertrude Spores, Lettie Whitaker, Mrs. Zook, Margaret Bettis, Lottie Whitaker, and Leona Spores. Second row, Ruth Mills, Ruby Taylor, Kathleen Maddox, unidentified, Ester Sherwood, and Thelma Lawrence. Third row, Emily Stoneberg, Roxy Riddle, Sarah Hoover, Clistie Meek, and Josie Gardner. *Courtesy Gladeus Simmons Pupke*

Below: The Standley family outside their home at 235 Mill Street in Eugene. The woman on the porch holding the baby is Lydia Standley. Henry Clay Standley is third from left. Photo circa 1910. *Courtesy Bray family*

Above: Junction City farm family, James and Amanda Rickard Calvert pose with their 12 children in this 1910 photo. James was born on the Row River near Cottage Grove and Amanda was the daughter of one of three brothers who came by wagon train and settled near Monroe. Eleven of the 12 children spent their lives in Lane County in Junction City, Thurston and Eugene; the 12th, a daughter, married a farmer and moved to the Shedd area of Linn County. Included in this photo are Ross, Grandpa Calvert, Tommy, Grandma, Iona, Katie, Rena, Avely, Ina, May, Stella, John, Evalina, and Roberta. *Courtesy Leonard J. Calvert*

Left: Theodore Roosevelt, former United States President, makes a "whistle stop" visit at Eugene railroad depot on his way to Portland, April 1911. *Courtesy Lane County Historical Museum*

Right: Methodist Episcopal Church on the east side of Willamette Street between 11th and 12 avenues, Eugene, 1913. This church was dedicated Easter Sunday, March 23, 1913. *Courtesy Lane County Historical Museum*

Left: Eugene Fire Department ladder wagon, circa 1910. This was Eugene's first paid fire department team. Driver on the left is Charlie Croner; on right is W.E. (Bill) Nusbaum, who succeeded Croner as fire chief. The horses are Flora and Ned. *Courtesy Donald P. Sales*

Below: Street improvement in Springfield, 1911. *Courtesy Springfield Museum*

Left: Eugene Fire Department team members with their new truck parked in front of the Eugene City Hall, circa 1913. The truck is identified as a Knott fire engine with ladders carried on top. The driver is Mr. Pennington. George Croner sits in uniform to his right; Billy Nusbaum is seated behind the driver. *Courtesy Lane County Historical Museum*

Right: Central Presbyterian Church Vacation Bible School students, Eugene, circa 1918. *Courtesy Central Presbyterian Church*

Above: Col. Jasper J. Harbaugh, constable and juvenile officer, in his office, Eugene, October 1920. *Courtesy Lane County Historical Museum*

Left: Harrisburg telephone and post office workers, 1917. Lady in dark dress is Ada Smith. This building once housed a bank and the building still stands across the street from the Vault Restaurant. *Courtesy Evelyn R. McGillivray*

Right: Members of the Eugene Police Department pose with their motorcycles and patrol wagon, 1920s. *Courtesy Lane County Historical Museum*

Above: Lane County Jail, 75 East 8th Avenue, circa 1926. *Courtesy Lane County Historical Museum*

Left: Interior or the Lane County Jail, circa 1926. *Courtesy Lane County Historical Museum*

Above: Ross M. and Florence Brooks Calvert at the time of their wedding in Junction City, 1925. *Courtesy Leonard J. Calvert*

Right: James and Amanda Calvert at their farm on their 50th wedding anniversary, October 24, 1925. The Junction City area farm was at the intersection of highways 36 and 99. *Courtesy Leonard J. Calvert*

Above: Publicity Committee for the first concert of the Eugene Gleemen, May 1926. Last names of these gentlemen, from left, Moody, Bell, Jones, Burnett, Jennings, Winder, Marshall and Leake. *Courtesy Eugene Gleemen Archives*

Below: Eugene Gleemen at the University of Oregon School of Music in Eugene, 1926. *Courtesy Eugene Gleemen Archives*

Above: Eugene Hospital at 1162 Willamette Street, circa 1927.
Courtesy Lane County Historical Museum

Left: Dare Devil Woods, the Human Fly, hangs from the top of the Eugene Hotel at 222 East 9th Avenue, July 26, 1928. *Courtesy Lane County Historical Museum*

Below: A crowd gathers on the Springfield Bridge to watch the flood waters flow by during the flood of 1927. *Courtesy Springfield Museum*

Community

Right: East 9th Street in Eugene during the flood of 1927. *Courtesy Springfield Museum*

Below: A flooded Gateway Service Station in west Glenwood, February 21, 1927. *Courtesy Springfield Museum*

Above: Gladeus Simmons, five-years old, 1929. *Courtesy Gladeus Simmons Pupke*

Above: Members of the Eugene Police Department pose on the steps of City Hall, June 10, 1927. *Courtesy Lane County Historical Museum*

Community

Right: Mabel Eidson, of Eugene, received the honor of being one of Oregon's outstanding girl club leaders. She won an airplane ride, a dinner with the governor and other prominent officials in 1930. She also received a gold watch and a week's outing at Crater Lake. *Courtesy Mabel Eidson Rear*

Above: Bray family photo, Eugene, circa 1927. Pictured from left to right are, Rex and Golda Reed (holding Bob). On couch, Jack and Dorothy Hodges, Ella and Orin Bray, Alvin Bray, Ethel and Walt White. At the table is Glenn Reed (previous mayor of Bend), and Betty Maycumber. *Courtesy Bray family*

Left: Unidentified individuals pose beside confiscated bootlegging equipment piled up on the grounds of the Lane County Courthouse at 125 East 8th Avenue Eugene, circa 1930. *Courtesy Lane County Historical Museum*

Right: Patsy Williams decked out for the Trails to Rails pageant in Eugene, 1937. *Courtesy Patricia Williams Jacobson*

Above: Construction of the United States Post Office at 538 Willamette Street, December 19, 1938. *Courtesy Lane County Historical Museum*

Left: George Northam, left, and his brother John sold papers at the corner of 9th and Willamette in Eugene from this wagon powered by a car battery, 1932. Tiny Drake, the boys' boss, built this wagon (one of two), with a car battery so the boys and potential customers could listen to music played on the radio he installed. The boys sold the Sunday Seattle P.I. and the Sunday San Francisco Chronicle from their wagon. During the week they sold The Eugene Register-Guard. *Courtesy John Northam*

Right: The Highway Baptist Church, Cottage Grove, circa 1939. *Courtesy Lane County Historical Museum*

CHAPTER EIGHT

Recreation & Celebration

Even in black-and-white photographs, Lane County's early parades and festivals are larger-than-life. These regular events raised quite the hubbub - engines idling, horses snorting, band music blaring and crowds cheering. Every city seemed to find a way to put on a Fourth of July parade, complete with flags, flowers and fair maidens.

These were the days of homegrown entertainment. From the fire department to the mayor, townsfolk turned out to celebrate holidays and their community.

Lifelike sets and props, handmade costumes and dozens of amateur actors put on reenactments - one included the fording of a river - that thrilled Lane County's pre-television audiences. Crowds also flocked to the Lane County Fair, which began in downtown Eugene in 1884. Circuses provided novel entertainment, although civic leaders urged citizens to watch their pocketbooks.

Behind many of the celebrations were the combined efforts of local social clubs. The first fraternal organization was the Masonic Lodge, established in 1856 in Eugene. The Independent Order of Odd Fellows debuted in 1860, and the Commercial Club — the local chamber of commerce — opened a site in 1903 that featured billiard and pool tables and a bowling alley. Women gathered for sewing circles and eventually founded the Fortnightly Club for social and cultural pursuits.

The novelty of the airplane captured the interest of old and young alike. Some of the best flying machines of the time came through Eugene's airport, which opened in 1919 as the first municipal airport on the Pacific Coast. In 1923, the first around-the-world flight crew landed there.

Traveling was a fine diversion from work. Residents could catch the train to Portland, visit hot springs on the eastern side of the county or take a trip to the coast. Those who wanted to travel back and forth between Eugene and Springfield boarded a new electric streetcar that crossed the Willamette River. After Eugene and Springfield took turns banning alcohol, the streetcar earned a reputation for the raucous behavior of riders returning home after a night's drinking.

Left: Shriner's Parade down Willamette Street, Eugene, September 5, 1908. *Courtesy Lane County Historical Museum*

Right: Seven girls on velocipedes (early tricycles) on the board walk in front of the Thomas G. Hendricks residence at the corner of Charnelton and West 9th Avenue in Eugene, circa 1890. *Courtesy Lane County Historical Museum*

Above: The T.G. Hendricks and F.M. Wilkins families pay a visit to Heceta Head, 1892. Horses and carriages are lined up the beach, which is now Devil's Elbow State Park. Notice one of the light keeper's residences is under construction at right. *Courtesy Lane County Historical Museum*

Right: Chester R. Chrisman poses with his bicycle in front of the steps to his home at 112 West 10th Avenue, Eugene, circa 1896. *Courtesy Lane County Historical Museum*

Above: A patriotic 1898 Fourth of July float in a parade in Junction City. The two girls standing wear "Goddess of Liberty" crowns. *Courtesy Lane County Historical Museum*

Left: "Dry Land Navy" float in the 1898 Fourth of July parade in Junction City. *Courtesy Lane County Historical Museum*

Recreation & Celebration

Left: Aletha and Pearl Morris in their goat cart, late 1800s. *Courtesy Lane County Historical Museum*

Below left: Eugene Fire Department's horse-drawn fire wagon all decked out for a parade, circa 1905. *Courtesy Marie Marshall*

Below: A July 4th parade on Willamette Street in front of the Hovey Block, Eugene, circa 1900. *Courtesy Lane County Historical Museum*

Right: A Shriner's parade on Willamette Street, Eugene, September 5, 1908. *Courtesy Lane County Historical Museum*

Left: Holmes Bros. baseball team, Springfield, early 1900s. Maude F. Bryan is pictured in the middle of the players. Those known, left to right, first row are Bill Chapin and Doug Rankin. Second row, Nels Skeele, unidentified, Wiley Humphrey and Jim Clark. *Courtesy Springfield Museum*

Above: The Sweet Pea parade on Main Street in Cottage Grove, July 8, 1910. *Courtesy Lane County Historical Museum*

Right: Fourth of July parade on Main Street, Cottage Grove, circa 1910. *Courtesy Lane County Historical Museum*

Right: Hunters, Jess and Vern Smith and Smith Mountjoy at Kelsey's hop yard, circa 1910. *Courtesy Springfield Museum*

Above: The bowling alley between 2nd and 3rd streets and south of Main Street, Springfield, 1910. *Courtesy Springfield Museum*

Left: The Pleasant Hill baseball team, including 27 members, poses in the field behind the W.O.W. Hall, Pleasant Hill. Pictured, left to right, standing are Virgil Cornelius, Lem Drury, Prof. Enlow, Lloyd Stratton, Prof. Hugg, Bent Matthews, Clint Shelley, L. Fred Furrow, Will Wheeler, Earnest Wheeler, Dave Linton, John Gilbert, Herman Miller, and C.C. Mulkey. Middle row, sitting are Sam Baughman, Charley Sherwood, John Shermer, and Ed Shelley. First row, Alta Stoops, Mark Young, Rob Baughman, George Lord, Arthur McKenzie, August Shermer, Dugle Rankin, and Arthur Satzer. *Courtesy Lane County Historical Museum*

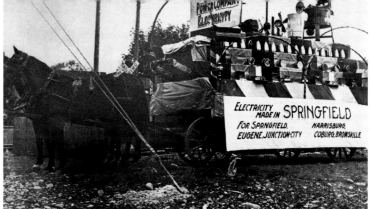

Above: Oregon Power Company, later known as Mountain States and then Pacific Power and Light, float in a parade advertising the service and electrical appliances of the company. Notice the electric irons, toasters and electric fans. *Courtesy Springfield Museum*

Left: Three Native American men seated in a flying machine at the 1912 Lane County Fair. If you look closer you can see this photo has been altered. *Courtesy Lane County Historical Museum*

Above: Springfield baseball team, 1913. In the photo are, Manager, L.M. Beebe; catcher, Smith; second base, Baird; left field, Wagers; first base, Blanchard; center field, Meats; short stop, Lechner; third base, Cairns; pitcher, Hewett; sub, Wilhelm; right field *Courtesy Springfield Museum*

Right: The Lane County Fair was the place to be for fun and food in 1911. This well-dressed family met in front of Henry Standley's popcorn wagon for a photo. The popcorn dispenser was Henry Lough. *Courtesy Lane County Historical Museum*

Above: McDonald Theatre at 1020 Willamette Street, Eugene, 1927. The marquee is advertising *Ali-din*, *The Man Who Knows* and Eddie Cantor in *Special Delivery*.   *Courtesy Lane County Historical Museum*

Left: Frank Spicer, seated at center, conducts the I.O.O.F. (Independent Order of Odd Fellows) band at an early 1920s Lane County Fair in Eugene.   *Courtesy Lane County Historical Museum*

Above: Bathing beauties at the Star Lumber Company mill pond near Dexter, circa 1922. Included in the photo are Willie Montgomery, Margie Larson, Litha Button, Mable Deaton Montgomery, Lillie Christenson and Lois Larson.   *Courtesy Patricia (Williams) Jacobson*

Right: A parade on Willamette Street, between 7th and 8th avenues on July 4th 1918.   *Courtesy Lane County Historical Museum*

Recreation & Celebration

Above: Burton Sisters Orchestra pose with their instruments in Eskimo costumes, Eugene, 1927. They were a local well-known family musical group. *Courtesy Lane County Historical Museum*

Left: National Guard soldiers advertising *Corporal Kate* in front of McDonald's Theatre at 1020 Willamette Street, Eugene, March 25, 1927. *Courtesy Lane County Historical Museum*

Above: Eugene youth line up for a bicycle race on July 1, 1927. *Courtesy Lane County Historical Museum*

Above: Horses and riders parade through crowd-lined streets in an Oregon Trail Pageant parade, Eugene, late 1920s. The pageant celebrations took place every few years from 1926-1950. *Courtesy Lane County Historical Museum*

Below: McMorran & Washburne Department Store's display at the fair, August 30, 1930. *Courtesy Lane County Historical Museum*

Right: Lady Newberry, an employee from J.J. Newberry Company Department Store, poses in costume for Trail-to-Rail Parade, circa 1930. *Courtesy Lane County Historical Museum*

Above: Oregon Trail Pageant parade heads south on Willamette Street, Eugene, circa 1929. *Courtesy Lane County Historical Museum*

Left: Lane County Fair booth promoting Maxwell House Coffee, Eugene, circa 1935. *Courtesy Lane County Historical Museum*

Right: First Oregon State ham radio convention in Eugene, circa 1932. *Courtesy Barbara Anheluk*

Above: Girls pose with their dogs in preparation for the Pet Parade in Eugene, circa 1930. *Courtesy Lane County Historical Museum*

Left: Crowds gather on West 8th Avenue for a Pet Parade in Eugene, circa 1930. *Courtesy Lane County Historical Museum*

Index